HAL•LEONARD

INSTRUMENTAL PLAY-ALONG

AUDIO ACCESS INCLUDED

PLAYBACK+
Speed • Pitch • Balance • Loop

TROMBONE

FAVORITE Disney SONGS

Audio arrangements by Peter Deneff

To access audio, visit:
www.halleonard.com/mylibrary

Enter Code
1160-4015-1488-2685

ISBN 978-1-70514-274-5

Visit Hal Leonard Online at
www.halleonard.com

Contact us:
Hal Leonard
7777 West Bluemound Road
Milwaukee, WI 53213
Email: info@halleonard.com

In Europe, contact:
Hal Leonard Europe Limited
42 Wigmore Street
Marylebone, London, W1U 2RN
Email: info@halleonardeurope.com

In Australia, contact:
Hal Leonard Australia Pty. Ltd.
4 Lentara Court
Cheltenham, Victoria, 3192 Australia
Email: info@halleonard.com.au

CONTENTS

THE BALLAD OF THE LONESOME COWBOY

from TOY STORY 4

TROMBONE

Music and Lyrics by
RANDY NEWMAN

rit.   a tempo

EVERMORE
from BEAUTY AND THE BEAST

TROMBONE

Music by ALAN MENKEN
Lyrics by TIM RICE

HOW DOES A MOMENT LAST FOREVER

from BEAUTY AND THE BEAST

TROMBONE

Music by ALAN MENKEN
Lyrics by TIM RICE

HOW FAR I'LL GO
from MOANA

TROMBONE

Music and Lyrics by
LIN-MANUEL MIRANDA

INTO THE UNKNOWN

from FROZEN 2

TROMBONE

Music and Lyrics by KRISTEN ANDERSON-LOPEZ
and ROBERT LOPEZ

IT'S ALL RIGHT

featured in SOUL

TROMBONE

Words and Music by
CURTIS MAYFIELD

LAVA
from LAVA

TROMBONE

Music and Lyrics by
JAMES FORD MURPHY

LEAD THE WAY
from RAYA AND THE LAST DRAGON

TROMBONE

Music and Lyrics by
JHENÉ AIKO

THE PLACE WHERE LOST THINGS GO

from MARY POPPINS RETURNS

TROMBONE

Music by MARC SHAIMAN
Lyrics by SCOTT WITTMAN and MARC SHAIMAN

NEVER TOO LATE

from THE LION KING 2019

TROMBONE

Music by ELTON JOHN
Lyrics by TIM RICE

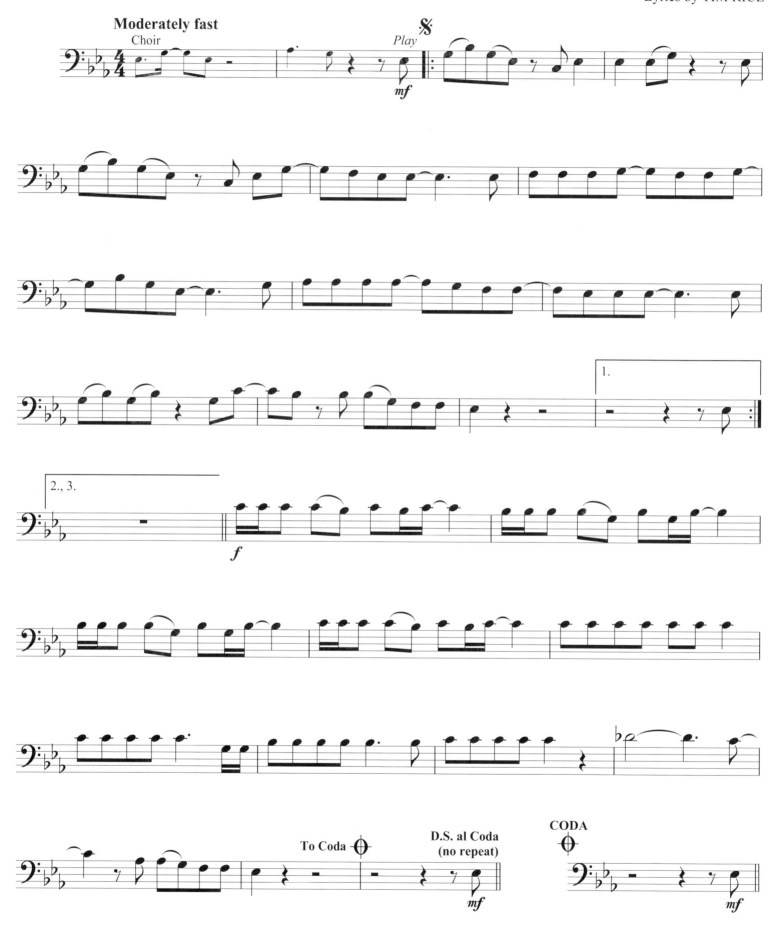

SPEECHLESS
from ALADDIN (2019)

TROMBONE

Music by ALAN MENKEN
Lyrics by BENJ PASEK
and JUSTIN PAUL

TOUCH THE SKY
from BRAVE

TROMBONE

Music by ALEXANDER L. MANDEL
Lyrics by ALEXANDER L. MANDEL
and MARK ANDREWS

TRY EVERYTHING

from ZOOTOPIA

TROMBONE

Words and Music by SIA FURLER,
TOR ERIK HERMANSEN and MIKKEL ERIKSEN

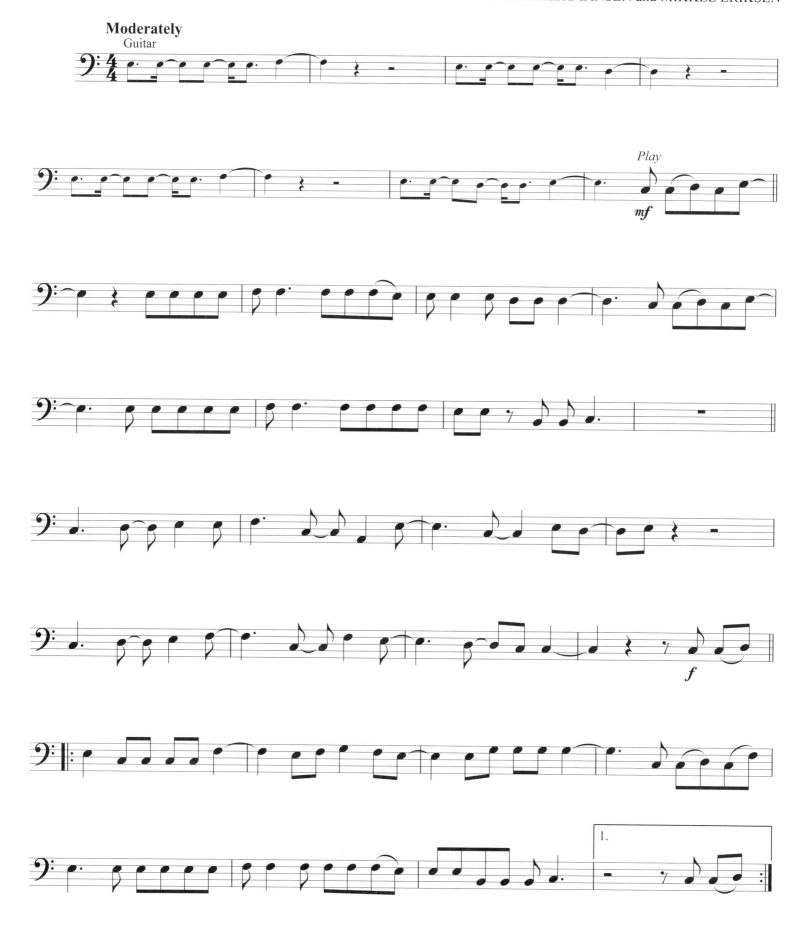

YOU'RE WELCOME

from MOANA

TROMBONE

Music and Lyrics by
LIN-MANUEL MIRANDA

REMEMBER ME
(Ernesto de la Cruz)
from COCO

TROMBONE

Words and Music by KRISTEN ANDERSON-LOPEZ
and ROBERT LOPEZ